VINTAGE VIBES
VOL. 2

A COLORING BOOK *for* ADULTS *and* CURIOUS CHILDREN

VINTAGE
HOLIDAY POSTCARDS

Jodie Randisi

ISBN 978-0-9960533-6-5

EST. COWCATCHER 1992
PUBLICATIONS
HILTON HEAD, SC

PRACTICAL AND ORNAMENTAL

Penmanship,

AS TAUGHT AND PRACTICED BY

DANIEL T. AMES.

Vintage Holiday Postcards Coloring Book
ISBN 978-0-9960533-5-8
Design by Steven Plummer, SPBookDesign.com
Graphics & illustrations, graphicsfairy.com, viintage.com, scrapgirls.com.

POST CARD

PLACE STAMP HERE

HOW TO GET THE RESULTS YOU WANT

Best practices would be to remove pages from the book and make photocopies for the purposes of resizing and mistakes. Permission is given to make copies for your personal use only. Copyright restriction prohibits reproduction for commercial use. No permission is given to share, sell, or disseminate these pages without written permission from the publisher.

If you choose to color with markers, please be aware of problems with ink bleeding through the paper.

When you want to create a homemade postcard, make a copy on white cardstock paper. Extra postage will be charge if your postcard exceeds postal regulations.

To qualify for the postcard mailing rate, you must adhere to
At least 3½" high by 5" long, no more than 4¼" high by 6" long.

VALENTINE'S DAY

"The best and most beautiful things in the world cannot be seen or even touched. They must be felt with the heart."

HELEN KELLER

To my Valentine

To my Valentine

POST CARD

POST CARD

A MESSAGE of TRUE LOVE.

A MESSAGE of TRUE LOVE.

POST CARD

POST CARD

Cupid's Message

Cupid's Message

POST CARD

PLACE STAMP
HERE

POST CARD

PLACE STAMP
HERE

Valentine Greeting

POST CARD

POST CARD

MY VALENTINE

MY VALENTINE

POST CARD

PLACE STAMP
HERE

POST CARD

PLACE STAMP
HERE

To·My·Valentine

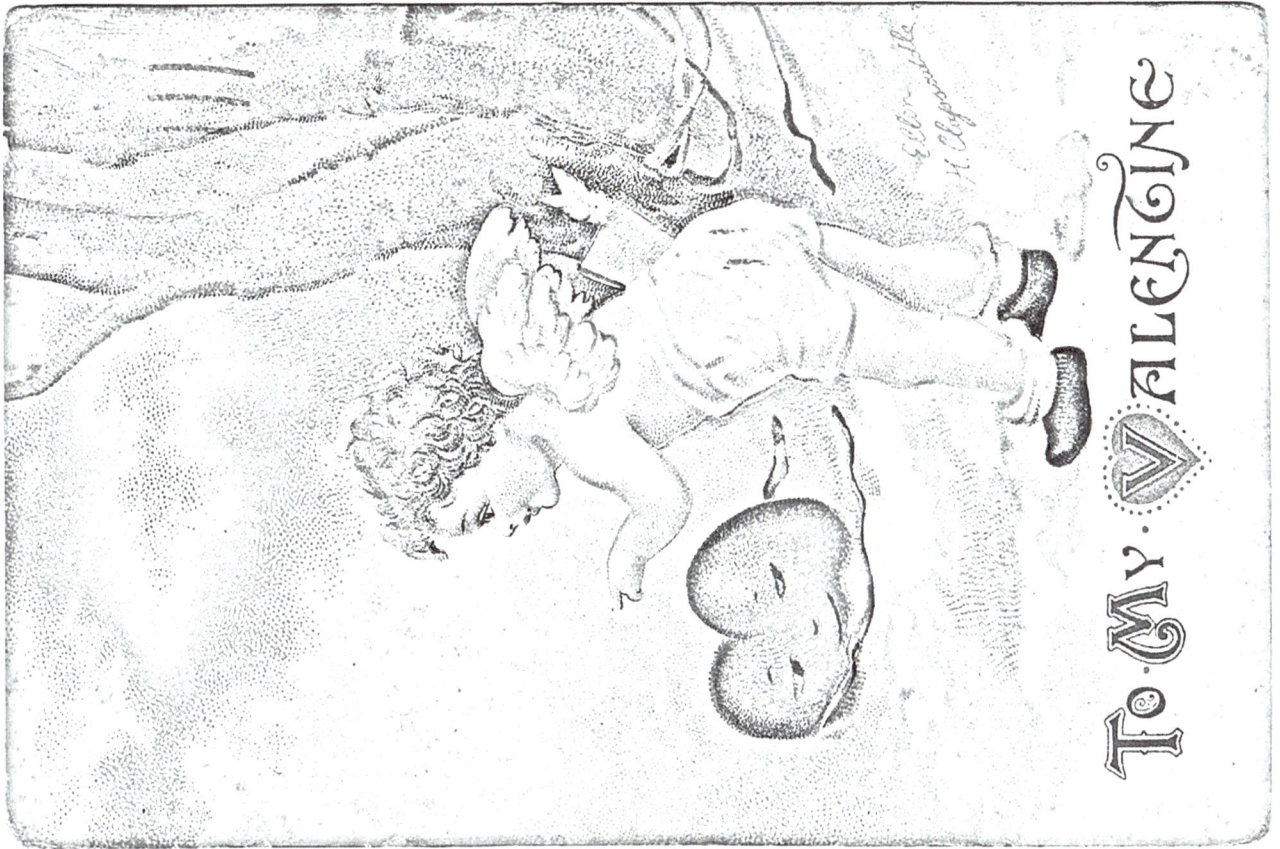

To·My·Valentine

POST CARD

PLACE STAMP
HERE

POST CARD

PLACE STAMP
HERE

To my Valentine

Don't drive a willing horse to death.

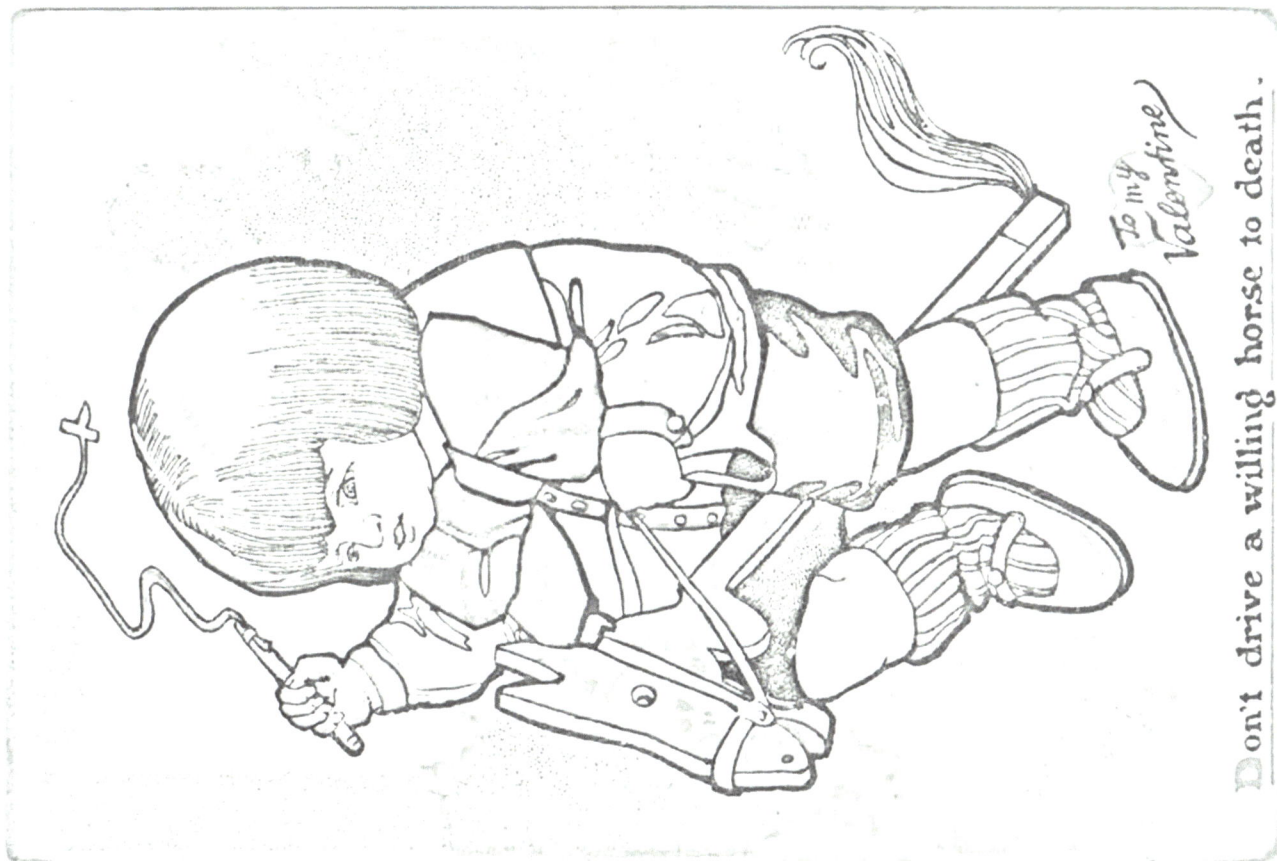

To my Valentine

Don't drive a willing horse to death.

POST CARD

PLACE STAMP
HERE

POST CARD

PLACE STAMP
HERE

POST CARD

POST CARD

To my Valentine.

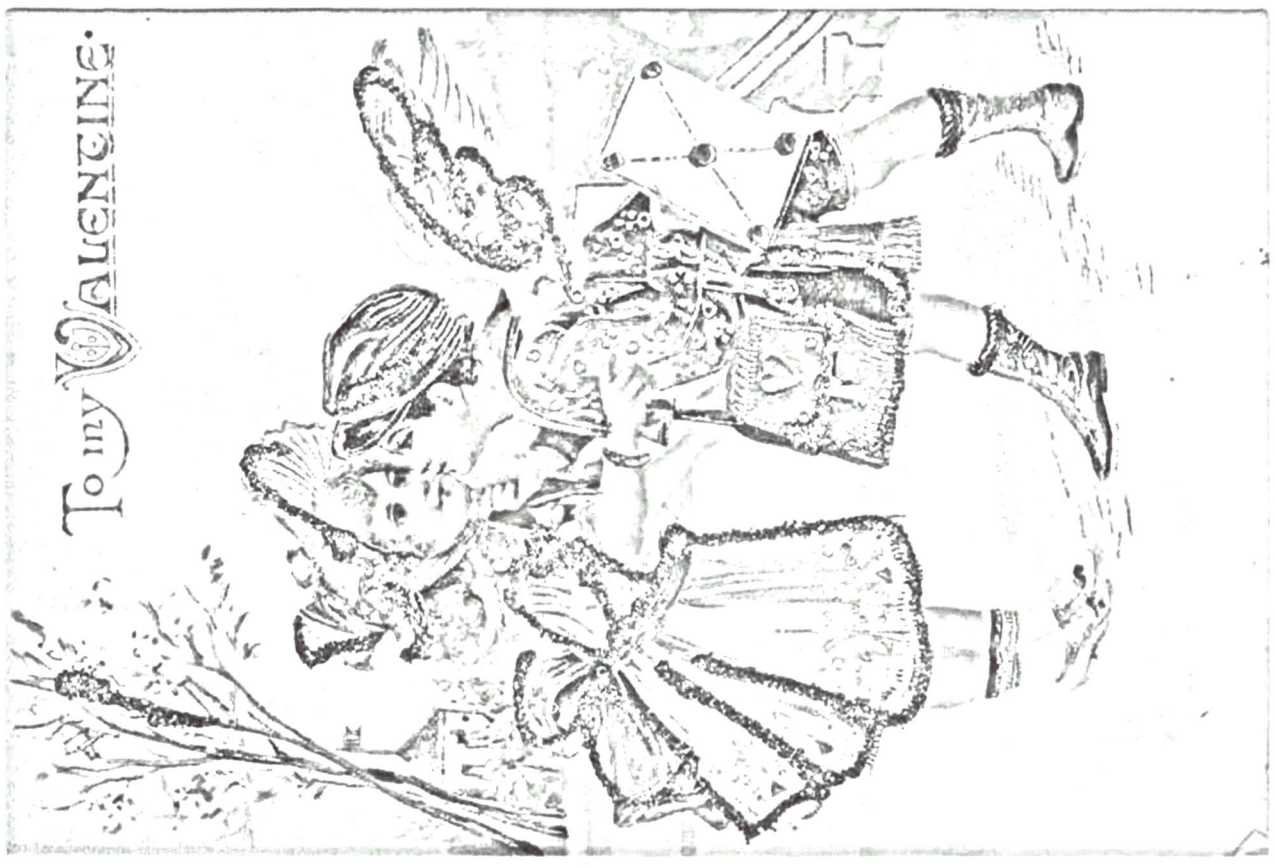

To my Valentine.

POST CARD

POST CARD

To my Valentine

To my Valentine

POST CARD

PLACE STAMP
HERE

POST CARD

PLACE STAMP
HERE

TO MY GALENTINE.

TO MY GALENTINE.

POST CARD

PLACE STAMP
HERE

POST CARD

PLACE STAMP
HERE

Isn't it Fun to
be
Sweethearts

Isn't it Fun to
be
Sweethearts

POST CARD

PLACE STAMP
HERE

POST CARD

PLACE STAMP
HERE

EASTER

"I am the resurrection and the life.
He who believes in me will live, even
though he dies; and whosoever lives
and believes in me will never die."

JOHN 11:25-26

Best Easter Wishes

Best Easter Wishes

POST CARD

PLACE STAMP
HERE

POST CARD

PLACE STAMP
HERE

Easter Greeting

Easter Greeting

POST CARD

PLACE STAMP
HERE

POST CARD

PLACE STAMP
HERE

A happy Easter

A happy Easter

POST CARD

PLACE STAMP
HERE

POST CARD

PLACE STAMP
HERE

POST CARD

PLACE STAMP
HERE

POST CARD

PLACE STAMP
HERE

POST CARD

POST CARD

THANKSGIVING

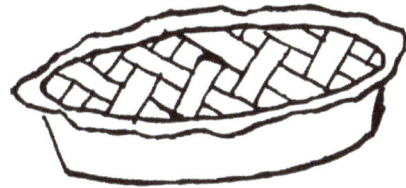

Give Thanks!

Best Wishes
for a Happy
Thanksgiving.

Best Wishes
for a Happy
Thanksgiving.

POST CARD

PLACE STAMP
HERE

POST CARD

PLACE STAMP
HERE

Cordial
Thanksgiving Greetings

Cordial
Thanksgiving Greetings

POST CARD

POST CARD

Thanksgiving Day

Thanksgiving Day

POST CARD

POST CARD

POST CARD

PLACE STAMP
HERE

POST CARD

PLACE STAMP
HERE

CHRISTMAS

merry &

Therefore the Lord himself shall give you a sign: The virgin will be with child and give birth to a son and he will be called Immanuel.

ISAIAH 7:14

bright

SUCCESS PROSPERITY GOOD WILL

X-MAS GREETINGS

HAPPINESS

SUCCESS PROSPERITY GOOD WILL

X-MAS GREETINGS

HAPPINESS

POST CARD

POST CARD

A Happy Christmas.

A Happy Christmas.

POST CARD

POST CARD

POST CARD

POST CARD

Joyous Christmas

Joyous Christmas

POST CARD

PLACE STAMP
HERE

POST CARD

PLACE STAMP
HERE

A Merry Christmas and a Bright New Year.

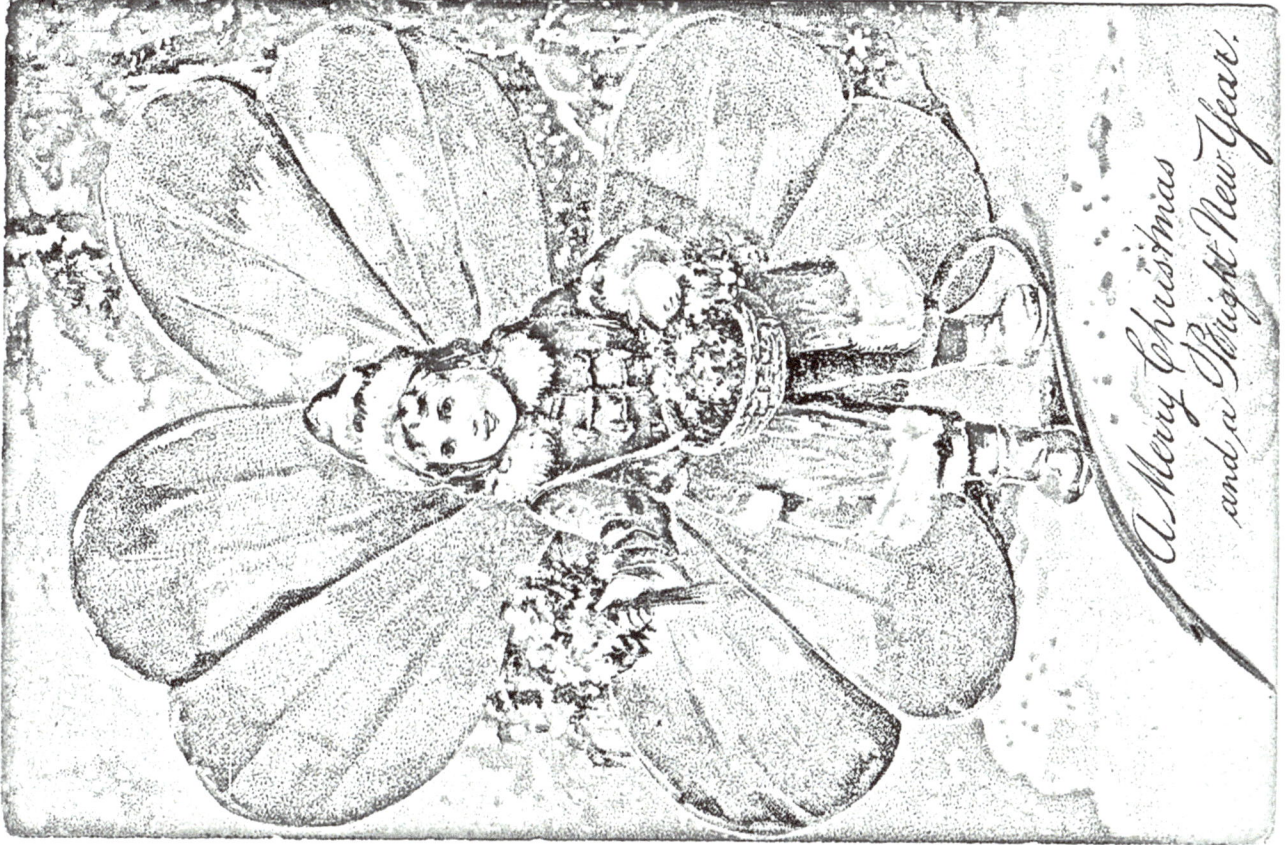

A Merry Christmas and a Bright New Year.

POST CARD

PLACE STAMP
HERE

POST CARD

PLACE STAMP
HERE

When Shepherds watched their Flocks by night

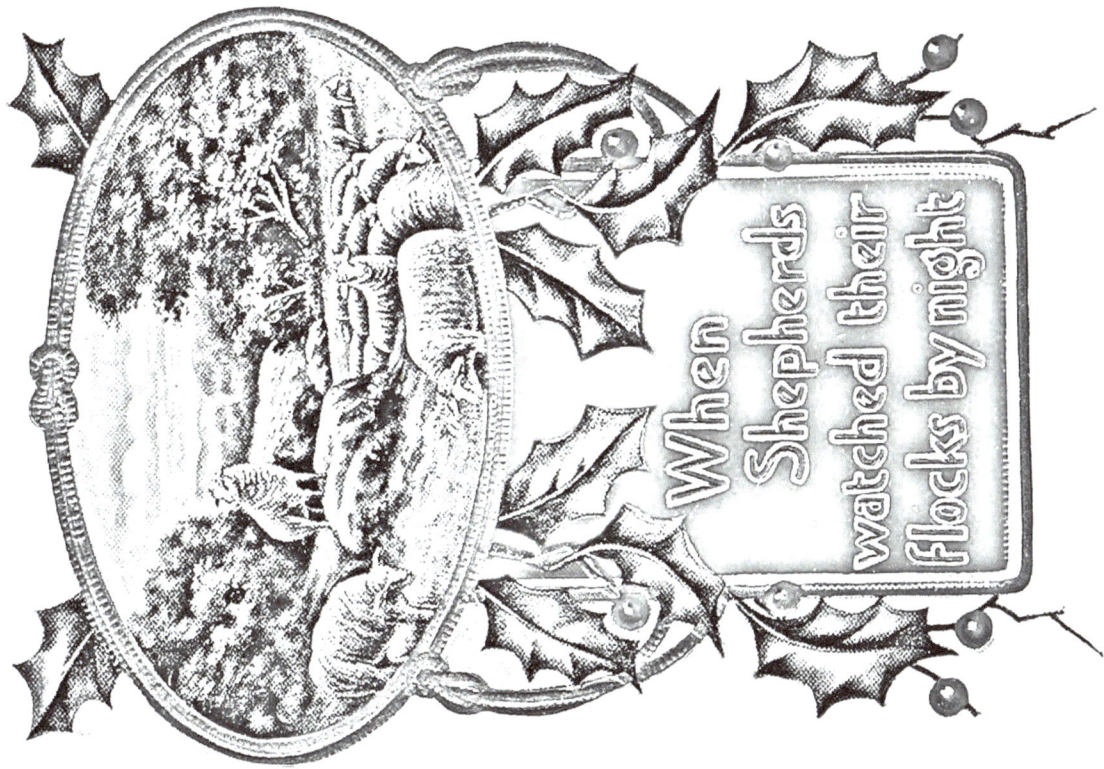

When Shepherds watched their Flocks by night

POST CARD

POST CARD

POST CARD

PLACE STAMP
HERE

POST CARD

PLACE STAMP
HERE

POST CARD

PLACE STAMP
HERE

POST CARD

PLACE STAMP
HERE

Christmas Wishes

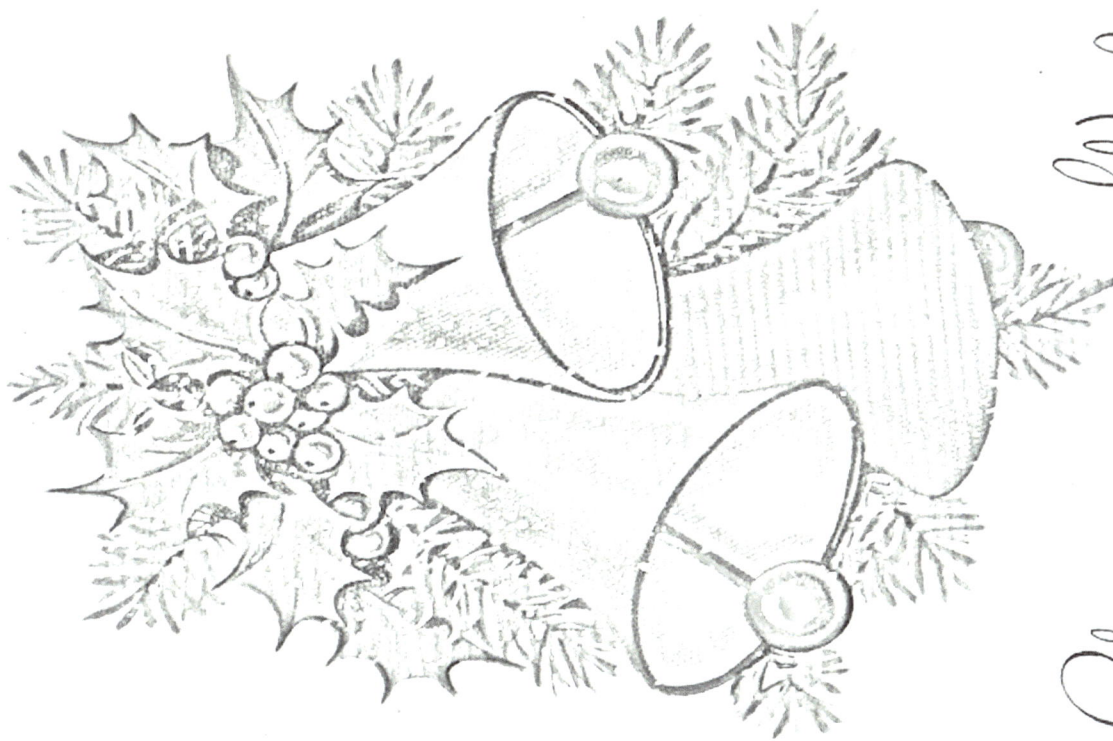

Christmas Wishes

POST CARD

PLACE STAMP
HERE

POST CARD

PLACE STAMP
HERE

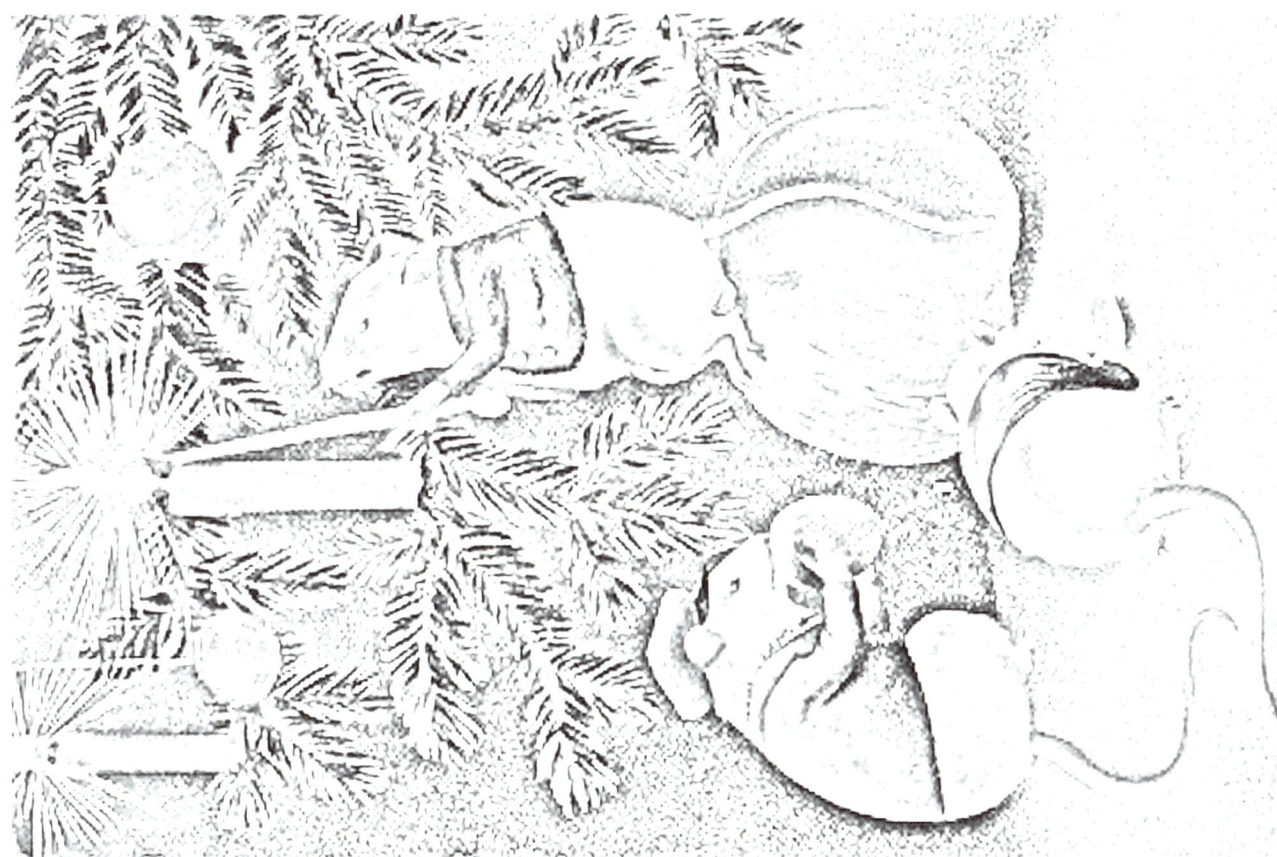

POST CARD

POST CARD

BEETON'S BOOK OF HOUSEHOLD MANAGEMENT

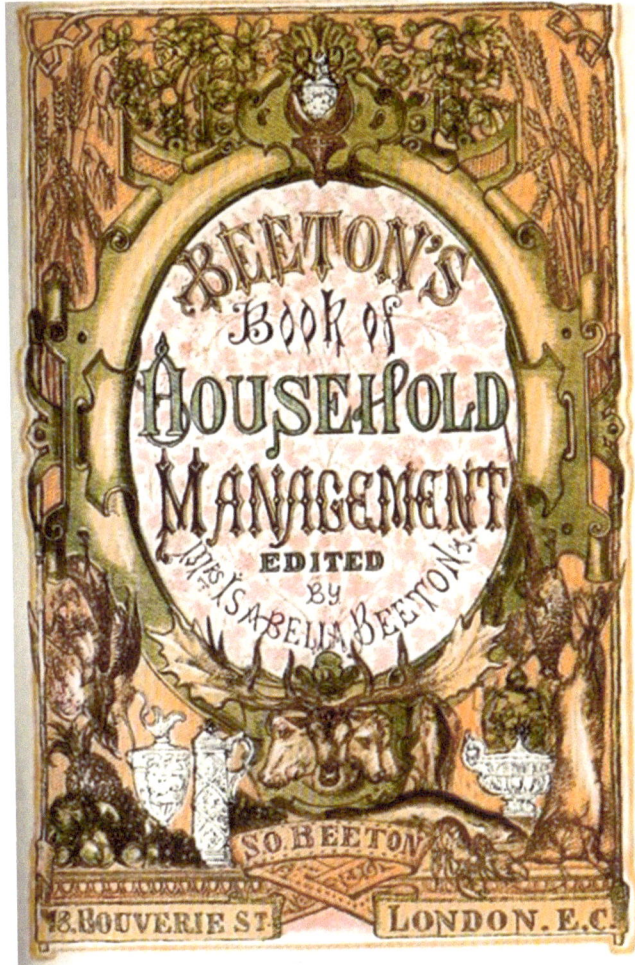

Written by what one might now describe as a Victorian Martha Stewart, these specially selected 14 illustrations served as a guide to running a household in Victorian Britain and are absolutely scrummy!

The author, Isabella Beeton, was 21 years old when she started working on her book. The book was initially serialized in 24 monthly installments, which were eventually collected into one volume under the title, **The Book of Household Management.** Mrs. Beeton's book became an immediate best-seller, selling 60,000 copies in its first year and totally nearly 2 million up to 1868.

Mrs. Beeton's book highlights the concerns of the ever-expanding Victorian middle class at a key moment in its history, and is so much fun to color.

An abridged edition is available on Amazon from Oxford's World Classics.

Mrs. Beeton has been described as
"the grandmother of modern domestic goddesses."

IMAGINE YOUR CREATION

in a attractive frame, perhaps displayed on a kitchen wall.

GIFT IDEA: Get the coloring book as well as the book on Amazon. Put them together with some coloring supplies and wrap with a vintage table cloth and bow.

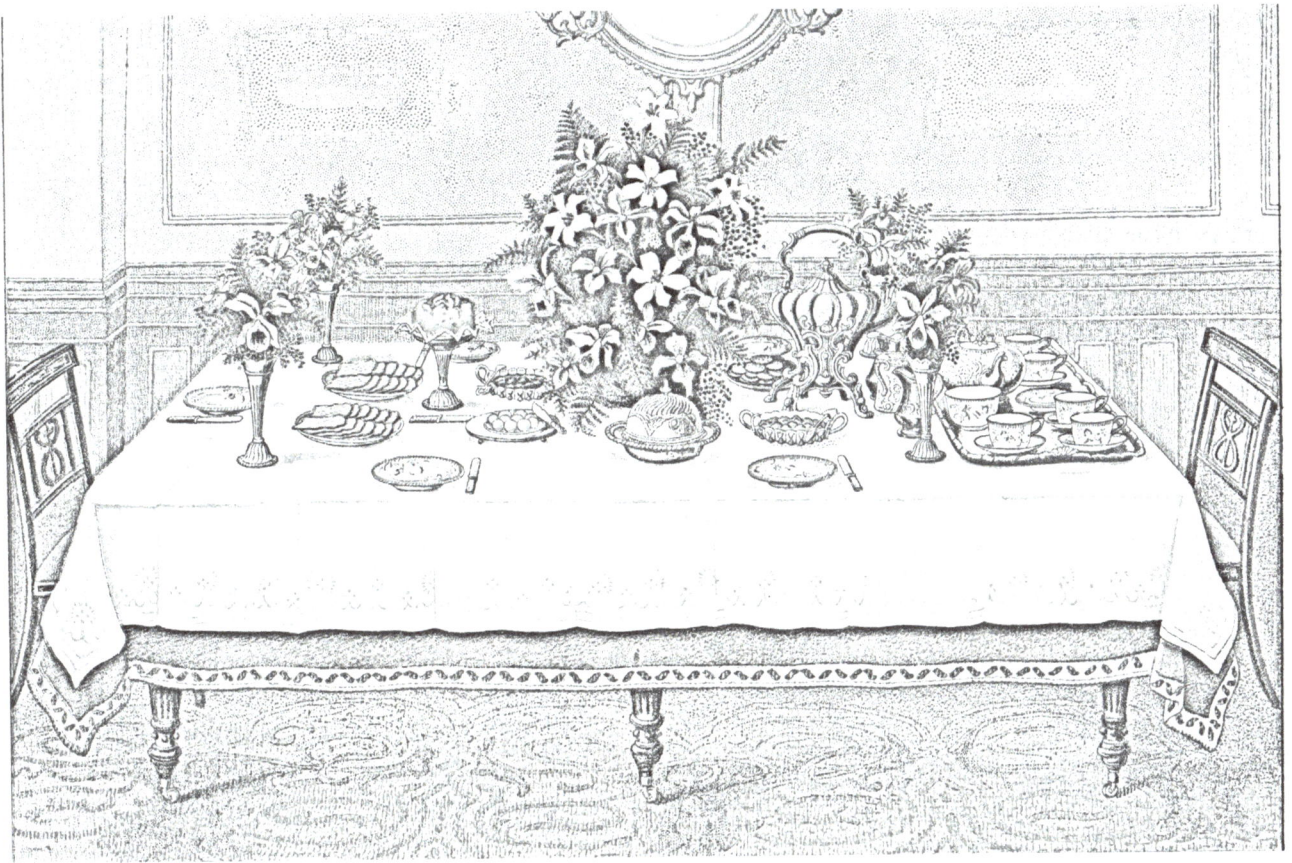

POST CARD

POST CARD

HOW TO GET THE RESULTS YOU WANT VIDEOS:

Coloring these pages is easier than it looks, especially when you know a few tricks.
Check out Jodie Randisi's Coloring Calling Santa video.

https://youtu.be/FfZQv1Z0VWA

TO SCHEDULE A COLORING WORKSHOP CONTACT:

jodie@coloringdepot.com.

EST. COWCATCHER 1992
PUBLICATIONS
HILTON HEAD, SC

This publication is available at a discount
when purchased in quantity to use as a
premium, sales promotion, in corporate
training programs, or by schools or
organizations for educational or
cause marketing purposes.

CONTACT

(843) 816-7883
jodie@coloringdepot.com

www.ingramcontent.com/pod-product-compliance
Lightning Source LLC
Chambersburg PA
CBHW040915100426
42737CB00042B/88